How To Be #1
Without Being A #2

JASON HOLIMAN

How To Be #1

Without Being A #2

DEDICATION

FOR RYAN, "THE LITTLE ENGINE THAT COULD."

How To Be #1

Without Being A #2

How To Be #1

Without Being A #2

CONTENTS

How To Be #1

Without Being A #2

FORWARD

I love the title of this booklet. I had the idea for it long before there was any content. To be fair, there isn't much content as far as word count, or the number of pages. It is the simplicity and brevity which I think brings clarity and concise delivery of the idea I wanted to convey.

In 2018, I was thumbing through a weighty text book on leadership, which a friend was reading in the course of acquiring his MBA. I had the thought that 'it can't be this difficult.' For years I have used a phrase that I apply to many situations, and that is, "Treat Everyone Like an Adult." I decided to write a "book" titled, "The #1 Rule For Dynamic Leadership," and there is only one line in the book. "Treat everyone like an adult." That literary masterpiece was mostly a proof of concept project as it relates to self-publishing, which everyone is doing now it seems. Want to learn left-handed underwater basket weaving?
There is probably a self-published book detailing the steps in minute detail. After the book was available on Amazon, I began to think more about the idea presented and if it were indeed the only practice needed to be a successful leader. However, treating someone like an adult is subjective and will mean something different for everyone.
Originally this "book" contained many different ideas and numerous concepts explaining how I thought this might be accomplished. Alas, I felt the message was diminished by my attempt to explain something that is already obvious and so I condensed those pages into what you will find on the next page. I ask that you continue with an open mind. I feel strongly the concept presented will change your life and those around you for the better. Or, perhaps you'll toss this book in the trash and curse yourself for wasting a few bucks on some crackpot who thought he had a valid idea. In either case, thanks for the money you spent. I'll use it wisely.

How To Be #1

Without Being A #2

1 DO THIS

TREAT EVERYONE AS AN EQUAL

TREAT EVERYONE AS AN EQUAL

TREAT EVERYONE AS AN EQUAL

TREAT EVERYONE AS AN EQUAL

TREAT EVERYONE AS AN EQUAL

SUMMARY

I FEEL A NOTE OF EXPLANATION IS IN ORDER, BEFORE I CONTINUE WITH A SUMMATION. IF I COULD HAVE WRITTEN ONE PAGE WITH ONE SENTENCE, I WOULD HAVE DONE SO. KINDLE DIRECT PUBLISHING USES A MINIMUM OF 24 PAGES TO ACCOMMODATE THE PUBLISHING ON DEMAND REQUIREMENTS. IT HAS TO DO WITH THE WAY A PAPERBACK IS BOUND AND PRINTED AND THERE ARE BLANK PAGES RESTRICTIONS AS WELL. SHOULD YOU EVER CONSIDER SELF PUBLISHING, DO PLENTY OF RESEARCH ON THE PLATFORM YOU CHOOSE TO USE. THAT BEING SAID, KDP IS RIDICULOUSLY EASY TO USE.

I CAN ALMOST HEAR SNORTS OF DERISION FROM SOME AND PERHAPS A FEW CHUCKLES AT THE PERCEIVED IDIOCY OF MY STATEMENT, THAT WE ARE ALL EQUALS. BEFORE YOU WALK AWAY, DO ONE LAST THING. A THOUGHT EXPERIMENT OF SORTS. EINSTEIN IS FAMOUS FOR HIS THOUGHT EXPERIMENTS AND FEW, IF ANY OF US ARE HIS EQUAL. PERHAPS YOU ARE A GENIUS, BUT I'M NOT PROPOSING EINSTEIN LEVEL THINKING, ONLY THIS. FOR 60 SECONDS, IMAGINE WHAT IT WOULD LOOK LIKE IF YOU ACTUALLY DID TREAT EVERYONE AS YOUR EQUAL. NOT LIKE AN EQUAL, BUT AS AN EQUAL.THERE IS AN IMPORTANT DISTINCTION BETWEEN THOSE TWO WORDS, "LIKE" AND "AS." LIKE, SEEMS TO IMPLY ONE IS PRETENDING TO SEE THE OTHER PERSON ON AN EQUAL FOOTING, WHILE AS, INDICATES AN ACTUAL BELIEF IN THE EQUALITY OF THE TWO. IF AFTER 60 SECONDS OF

SINCERE ANALYSIS, YOU DON'T SEE HOW DRAMATIC AN AFFECT THIS WAY OF THINKING AND BEHAVING WILL PRODUCE, THEN THIS CONCEPT ISN'T FOR YOU. FOR EVERYONE ELSE WHO PAUSED IN SERIOUS REFLECTION, THE JOURNEY HAS JUST BEGUN. A CERTAIN AMOUNT OF HUMILITY IS REQUIRED TO SEE, FEEL, OR ACT ON THE BELIEF, THAT EVERYONE IN YOUR WORLD IS YOUR EQUAL. I WON'T ATTEMPT TO EXPLAIN WHAT I THINK ANY OF THAT WOULD LOOK LIKE OR THE RESULTS I WOULD EXPECT TO SEE, BECAUSE EVERY SINGLE ONE OF US IS LIVING A DIFFERENT PATH AND THE RESULTS WILL BE AS VARIED AS WE OURSELVES ARE VARIED FROM ONE ANOTHER.

AT THE CORE OF THIS ACTION IS THE PHILOSOPHY THAT WE ARE ALL ONE. THE VERY ESSENCE OF WHO WE ARE, ORIGINATES FROM THE SAME SOURCE. YOU CAN CALL IT WHAT YOU WANT, MOST CALL IT GOD, SPIRIT, HIGHER POWER AND COUNTLESS OTHER THINGS. YET, EACH ONE POINTS TO ALL THE OTHERS AND TO ALL OF US. WHAT YOU SEE IN YOURSELF, IS WHAT YOU SEE IN OTHERS. SEE THE GOOD IN YOURSELF AND IT WILL BE REFLECTED BACK. YOUR IMAGE IN THE MIRROR DOESN'T SMILE FIRST. IF YOUR LIFE ISN'T ALL THAT YOU WISH FOR, KNOW THAT IT IS ONLY REFLECTING BACK AT YOU, WHAT YOU ARE PRESENTING TO THE WORLD.

PICK A DAY AND MARK IT ON YOUR CALENDAR. FOR 21 DAYS, PRACTICE THIS PHILOSOPHY. OLD HABITS WILL PREVAIL AT TIMES, BUT REDOUBLE YOUR EFFORTS TO SEE AND TREAT OTHERS AS YOUR ABSOLUTE EQUAL. IF AFTER 21 DAYS, YOUR LIFE ISN'T RADICALLY ALTERED, I'LL REFUND YOUR MONEY AND COME MOW YOUR GRASS OR SOMETHING. JUST KIDDING. I ALREADY SPENT THE MONEY AND I LOATHE YARD WORK.

THERE WILL BE SOME BLANK PAGES TO FOLLOW SO YOU CAN SKIP THOSE, UNLESS YOU ARE A DOODLER AND HAVE SOME FREE TIME.

How To Be #1

Without Being A #2

ABOUT THE AUTHOR

JASON HOLIMAN IS A FATHER OF TWO BOYS
AND A CAREER FIREFIGHTER OF 19 YEARS.

How To Be #1

Without Being A #2

CAN'T HAVE TOO MANY BLANK PAGES IN A ROW. SO HERE'S THIS.

YOU PROBABLY KNOW SOMEONE WHO COULD USE THE ADVICE OFFERED HERE. CONSIDER GIVING THEM A COPY.

CONSIDER PURCHASING MY OTHER BOOK. IT'S JUST AS WELL WRITTEN AS THIS ONE IS.

"WE DON'T GET WHAT WE WANT, WE GET WHAT WE ARE."

DR. WAYNE DYER

WE'RE ALL DONE HERE.
DON'T FORGET TO PASS THIS ALONG.
I RECOMMEND YOU DO IT ANONYMOUSLY.
I SUSPECT SOME PEOPLE WON'T LIKE IT MUCH, BUT
HONESTLY, THAT'S FUN TOO.

How To Be #1

Without Being A #2

www.ingramcontent.com/pod-product-compliance
Lightning Source LLC
Chambersburg PA
CBHW081653220526
45468CB00009B/2630